"SIMPLE"
LIFE SKILLS
FOR
TEENS SUCCESS

Easily Unlock Your Potential, Build Confidence and Resilience using Proven Strategies and Techniques

Dr. Fanatomy.

© Copyright 2023 - All rights reserved.

The content contained within this book may not be reproduced, duplicated or transmitted without direct written permission from the author or the publisher.

Under no circumstances will any blame or legal responsibility be held against the publisher, or author, for any damages, reparation, or monetary loss due to the information contained within this book, either directly or indirectly.

Legal Notice:
This book is copyright protected. It is only for personal use. You cannot amend, distribute, sell, use, quote, or paraphrase any part, or the content within this book, without the author or publisher's consent.

Disclaimer Notice:
Please note the information contained within this document is for educational and entertainment purposes only. All effort has been executed to present accurate, up-to-date, reliable, complete information. No warranties of any kind are declared or implied. Readers acknowledge that the author is not engaged in the rendering of legal, financial, medical or professional advice. The content within this book has been derived from various sources. Please consult a licensed professional before attempting any techniques outlined in this book.

By reading this document, the reader agrees that under no circumstances is the author responsible for any losses, direct or indirect, that are incurred as a result of the use of the information contained within this document, including, but not limited to, errors, omissions, or inaccuracies.

Bonus Booklet For You!

With great pleasure, I extend a warm welcome to you on your purchase of the book in this TeeNavigator series. Congratulations on stepping towards improving yourself and developing the skills necessary to thrive as a teenager and beyond.

Below is a surprise gift for you!

Download it from the link (or scan the QR code below) -
https://bit.ly/TeeNavigationBonus

Table of Contents

Introduction

Chapter 1: Healthy Habits for a Better You

Chapter 2: Master the Art of a Progressive Mindset

Chapter 3: The Financially Savvy Teen

Chapter 4: From Dreaming to Doing

Chapter 5: Developing Healthy Social Connections

Chapter 6: Home Maintenance 101

Chapter 7: Super Teen Role models

Chapter 8: Quiz Time

Conclusion

References

INTRODUCTION

Welcome to the teenage years! If you have just crossed the age of 12, you have reached a stage that may seem quite weird, different, and unlike any change, you've experienced. It is a time that confuses most — not just those changing but also those around them.

Teenagers are neither completely grown up nor are they kids anymore. They are in a sort of limbo age of their existence. This can be quite an annoying and frustrating experience. This explanation probably sounds like a trope or a cliché of every teenage character you might have come across in shows and movies. Well, even if it is new and plenty is changing, buckle up for the ride of a lifetime! There is a lot to learn in this phase, it can help you grow into a better and honest person later. You are responsible for yourself and should learn some basic skills to help you later. Teenage is important because it gives you an invaluable opportunity to mold yourself as you desire, along with chasing your goals.

This book can help you become a better person. It will offer simple and practical suggestions that can be used to transform your teenage experience!

So let us begin!

Dr. Fanatomy

1. Healthy Habits for a Better You

Nutrition, Personal Health, and Grooming

As we grow, we start making different decisions about different things. These are all decisions from what to wear, whom to meet, and where to go to more significant ones such as deciding the line of work. These decisions also include some related to your body and health. Making proper grooming, nutrition, and personal health decisions is necessary for a healthy body and a sound mind.

NUTRITION

Energy

Your body needs the energy to grow and function. This energy is received from the foods you consume in the form of calories. Different people need different amounts of calories to function. Excess calories can lead to obesity, while a lack of calories and nutrients can lead to malnutrition.

However, all calories are not the same. Some are good, and others are bad. For instance, even if the calories present are the same in a burger and a big salad bowl, only one is healthy. Making poor food choices and opting for foods rich in unhealthy calories does your body no favors. It also doesn't offer the energy needed.

Managing Weight

A healthy way to lose or gain weight is through proper exercise and nutrition. Excessive fasting, eating very little, cutting out certain groups of foods, skipping meals, smoking, using diet pills, bulimia, etc., are all wrong approaches to losing weight. Unhealthy weight loss methods may lead to malnourishment and other severe diseases and disorders.

It can also increase the chance of cancer, heart disease, and other health issues. Understand that you cannot be healthy if you don't take care of your body. If you want to lose or gain weight, it is recommended to contact a health professional who will guide you through the process.

Healthy Food

Healthy eating is not just about the quantity of food but also the quality and nutritional value of the food. It is recommended to avoid foods that are high in unhealthy fats, sugar, and salt and instead eat whole grains, vegetables, protein-rich food, and low-fat foods. Here are some examples of different groups of healthy foods that must be a part of your daily diet.

(a) Fruits and Vegetables

Half of your plate should consist of fruits. This is because red, dark green, and orange veggies have significant amounts of necessary nutrients such as calcium, vitamin C, and fiber.

(b) Grains

Whole grain products such as bread, oatmeal, brown rice, cereal, etc., should be used instead of white bread, white rice, etc.

(c) Protein

Instead of unhealthy protein sources, try lean and low-fat meats such as chicken or turkey. Other healthy protein sources include egg whites, seafood, nuts, beans, and tofu. Milk and dairy products are excellent sources of protein. If you are lactose intolerant, try soy milk with added calcium instead of regular milk.

(d) Fats

Many people believe that fat is a dangerous thing that must be removed from one's diet. This is false. Fat is integral to any diet as it helps your body develop and grow. It can also help to keep your skin and hair healthy.

Some fats are better than others. Sources of healthy fats include olives, avocados, nuts, seeds, and seafood, including tuna and salmon. Solid fats such as stick margarine, butter, and lard contain high amounts of trans and saturated fats, which are unhealthy.

(e) Minerals

Your body needs certain minerals such as sodium, calcium, zinc, and so on for proper functioning. Avoid consuming too much sodium, as it can be unhealthy for your body and heart. It is recommended to consume no more than 1 tsp of sodium daily. Processed and junk food are full of salt and sodium, so consuming them as little as possible is recommended. Instead of salt, you can use herbs and spices to flavor the meals.

Control your food portions

A portion of food or beverage is the amount you consume at once. Most consume larger portions than required, especially when eating out. Avoid overeating and consume only the necessary amount to power your body and mind.

Get Moving

Along with eating, physical activity should be an important part of your daily life. It does not matter what kind of physical activity you do — it should be vigorous and help you break a sweat. Regular physical activity, such as walking, biking, workout in the gym, etc., will strengthen your muscles and bones. It also improves your flexibility.

It is recommended to be physically active for at least 60 minutes daily. The activity can be moderate to vigorous. Engaging in vigorous or intense aerobic activity thrice a week is recommended. Aerobic activities or activities that make you breathe harder include biking, jogging, dancing, etc.

For moderate workouts, you can perform activities such as jogging, running, walking, or biking on a flat surface. To make the workout more intense, walk or run on slopes. Don't worry if you cannot work out for 60 minutes at a stretch; you can easily break down the time into multiple sessions. It is recommended to include some physical activity that can strengthen your muscles. This includes lifting weights, body-weight exercises, etc. Well, the exercise by no means is restricted to the options mentioned above. Daily chores such as taking out the trash, cleaning your house, walking your dog, etc., may not get your heart racing like jogging or biking.

Still, these activities are a great way to add some sort of activity to your routine. If you like a specific sport or want to learn one, go ahead and do it. The idea is to get your body moving.

Install a fitness app that can track your burnt calories and the number of steps to keep yourself active and accountable.

Have fun with your friends.

You don't have to be alone to be active. You can have fun with people such as your friends and family members. Find friends who can make you active. You can mix things up by choosing different activities every day. You can try sports or games such as tag, kickball, and other activities. Involve your friends and ask them to sign up for various activities with you.

PERSONAL HYGIENE

Dear teen, diet and physical exercise are just two parts of a healthy routine. For overall health, engaging in various personal hygiene activities is necessary.

It is necessary for everyone, including teens, to learn the basics of personal hygiene, as it can help you maintain good health. Personal hygiene is a set of activities or practices that should be performed regularly to keep the body clean and mind healthy. Apart from this, here are some other reasons why personal hygiene matters.

- Maintaining good personal hygiene will make you more comfortable in social settings. This helps boost your self-esteem and confidence and motivates you to lead a healthy and happy life. It also helps adjust to society and adulthood's norms, as personal hygiene is an important part of one's personality.

- It helps maintain cleanliness and avoid exposure to infections and diseases. For instance, cleanliness during menstruation helps teenage girls prevent any potential infections. Similarly, proper oral hygiene reduces the chances of developing cavities, bad breath, and gum problems.

- During adolescence, the human body undergoes various changes. These include increased body odor, hair growth, menstruation, etc. A proper hygiene routine keeps your body clean and prevents body odor.

- It also helps you stay focused on your goals and maintain discipline.

Types of Personal Hygiene for Teenagers

Personal hygiene is a term that encompasses a variety of meanings. It includes washing hands, bathing, brushing teeth and hair, etc. Below are some of the fundamental practices that will help maintain personal hygiene.

Hair care

Greasy hair and skin are among the most common issues these days. Teenagers are some of the most outgoing people in society. Due to this, their skin and hair tend to get quite dirty. Along with this, other internal changes such as hormonal changes, the skin and hair of teenagers tend to get oily and dirty. If the hair is thick, the problem becomes even more prominent. This is why it is necessary to wash your hair at least twice a week with a mild shampoo.

However, avoid washing your hair more than needed because it damages the natural oils released by the scalp and results in brittle hair. You may also use different hair care products — natural, store-bought, or homemade to enhance the quality of the hair. It is also recommended to consult a trichologist for any problems related to hair.

Skincare

Teenagers often face many different problems with their skin. The skin tends to get oilier during puberty. Oily skin traps dirt and dust and increases the risk of infections. These infections may lead to various skin issues, including blackheads, acne, etc. So, develop and maintain a proper and suitable skincare routine and wash your face regularly with mild soap. Use a gentle face cleanser, moisturize regularly, and don't forget about sunscreen when heading outdoors. Don't hesitate to consult a dermatologist if you have any severe and persistent problems. A skin doctor could provide appropriate skincare products and routines to treat skin troubles.

Nail care

Nowadays, most teens prefer to grow their nails and style them in different shapes, designs, and colors. Fingernails are, unfortunately, the perfect breeding ground for microbes. These microbes can then transfer from your nails to your mouth while eating.

9

They can also settle into your eyes, mouth, nose, eyes, and skin through touch. So, taking care of your nails is needed. This is much more than getting a mani-pedi. Ideally, scrub any dirt off your hands and nails using a brush. Wash your hands regularly to prevent the accumulation of dirt, dust, and microbes. It is also recommended to clip the nails regularly to avoid dirt and ingrown nails, which can be quite painful.

Oral care

Poor oral hygiene leads to tooth decay, gum diseases, and bad breath. It is necessary to brush and floss at least twice a day. It is also recommended to rinse the mouth with water after every meal. You may also use mouthwash to do the same.

Washing hands

Hands, due to their flexibility and accessibility, spread germs to almost all body parts. So, don't forget to wash your hands regularly before and after a meal. In addition, teens should ideally wash their hands after coming back from outside, playing with pets, using the washroom, or in any other situation where they may come in contact with a contaminated surface.

Bathing

A new type of sweat gland develops during puberty, making body odor quite common. These glands are present in the genital areas and armpits. Sweat is not smelly, but it acts as fodder for different types of bacteria that release compounds causing body odor.

So, teen or not, ensure you bathe daily and after vigorous physical activity. This removes sweat and bacteria that feed on sweat and, thus, prevents body odor. Antiperspirants can be used to control the production of sweat. Also, smelling good is a bonus of bathing regularly!

Toilet hygiene

This is generally just a reiteration of childhood practices that should be revisited and revised if necessary. Ensure that you clean and wipe your genitals after using the bathroom.

Menstrual hygiene

It is necessary for teens that menstruate to learn about their cycle and the care associated with it. They should learn to track their periods, use hygiene products such as tampons, sanitary napkins, and diva cups, and discard them safely. Menstrual hygiene is as important as any other advice discussed in this section.

Shave safe

During puberty, the body undergoes significant changes — one of which is the development of thick and coarse hair on various body parts. If you desire to shave off your beard, mustache, underarm hair, pubic hair, etc., it is recommended to buy a mild shaving cream and a safety razor. It is recommended that a parent or a guardian teach the teen how to shave without inflicting wounds. Teens, regardless of their gender, must understand the importance of sterilized shaving equipment and be careful while shaving delicate parts.

Teens should be taught about the after-shave skincare routine. You should never share your razor and other paraphernalia related to shaving with others.

Clean clothes and shoes

Changing your clothes every day is necessary. If it is impossible to change all your clothes, it is at least necessary to change your undergarments and socks daily.

Clothes retain and harbor germs, sweat, skin cells, and bodily fluids. You can counter problems such as smelly feet and body odor by wearing clean shoes and clothes.

Most of the suggestions discussed in this section might sound obvious. However, it is time to become conscious of your hygiene and make the needed changes. Teenage is the right time to develop healthy habits that will serve you well later.

Why Do Teens Face Personal Hygiene Issues?

There are different reasons why teens may face personal hygiene issues. Some of these reasons have been elaborated upon here.

Procrastination

Personal hygiene practices may seem boring because they are mundane and repetitive. This is why most tend to ignore or avoid them. There might have been days when you tried to postpone or avoid brushing their teeth, hair, or taking a bath, especially if you were not planning to go out or meet anyone.

You might avoid washing their hands after using the loo or before eating. Well, it is time to avoid them. Complete any task that takes a few minutes if you do it right away. This helps develop healthy habits and makes you feel better about yourself.

Lack of awareness

Another significant reason teens tend to be disinterested in personal hygiene is a lack of awareness. If teens are not aware of the importance of hygiene, they may tend to disregard the practices completely.

Cognitive and mental health problems

Some teens find it difficult to practice personal hygiene due to cognitive development delays.

Others also find it difficult to follow personal hygiene practices if they suffer from mental health problems like depression. In such cases, the teens either do not feel like engaging in personal hygiene practices or are unable to understand the importance of the same.

It is recommended that anyone with such problems must consult a medical professional immediately. They will help overcome these problems and impart the importance of a hygiene regimen. It is also advisable to consult therapists and counselors for the same.

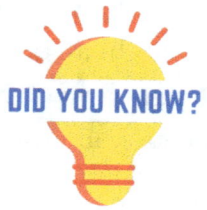

DID YOU KNOW?

- The brain continues to develop and grow until the age of 25.

- Adequate hydration helps to improve focus and concentration.

- A balanced diet that includes fruits, vegetables, whole grains, and lean protein can help improve mood and energy levels.

- Skipping breakfast can lead to overeating later in the day.

- Getting regular exercise can help improve sleep quality.

- Using too much shampoo or conditioner can strip the scalp of natural oils.

- Sleeping on your back can help reduce the appearance of wrinkles and prevent breakouts.

- Consuming sugary drinks can lead to weight gain and an increased risk of developing cavities.

- Brushing and flossing twice daily can help prevent gum disease and maintain oral health.

- Regular hand washing can help prevent the spread of illness and reduce the risk of infection.

2. MASTER THE ART OF A PROGRESSIVE MINDSET

How to Develop Winning Mindset?

Imagine this situation;

you worked hard and put great effort into an essay for school. You were sure you aced the essay but received a lower grade. How will you feel?

Does it mean there is scope for learning and improvement? Or will you feel bad and believe you cannot get the desired results regardless of your hard work?

If it is the former, it shows a growth mindset, whereas the latter doesn't. Are you wondering why it matters? Your mindset plays a significant role in life. Your thoughts and thinking patterns shape your mindset. This, in turn, influences how you view yourself, others, and life.

A negative or unhelpful mindset will hold you back, whereas a progressive or winning mindset will help you achieve the goals desired.

In this chapter, you will explore some methods, techniques, and tips to ensure you have a progressive mindset.

Connecting With Thought Leaders

Thought leaders are important leaders in any area of expertise or industry. It is necessary to connect with them, even though they may seem inaccessible. Here are a few ideas on how you can connect with thought leaders.

Objective

Instead of approaching a thought leader randomly, could you confirm your objective and understand why you want to connect with them? It is necessary to be clear about your goals before you decide to connect with any thought leader.

Know them and let them know you

You need to be visible around them so they can notice you. Most thought leaders are loyal to certain social media platforms and try to increase their presence on the social media platform they follow. Learn their preferences. Follow the leader wherever they go.

Manage your social profile

When you try to connect with thought leaders, it is necessary to keep your social media profile in place. It would help if you seemed professional, consistent, compelling, and unique.

Find identical connection points

To connect with a thought leader, try to find common ground between you and the leader. This will allow them to understand you better and connect with you efficiently.

Look out for all the things that are common between you two. Common connections are an asset for networking.

Conversation:
Merely following the thought leader is not enough; you must learn to communicate with them.

Social interactions and actions are essential. You can comment and share their content to open a channel of conversation. Do not barge into their inbox unless you have something crucial to say or ask.

Be thankful :
Nothing is more unappealing than appearing to be ungrateful and thankless. It is recommended to stand out and sincerely convey your thanks. You can customize your gratitude so the thought leader knows you appreciate their help.

Stay Connected :
Do not disappear after your work is done. Refrain from allowing your relationship with the thought leader to be purely transactional. Try to nurture the relationship and continue with it in reality and online.

Be real
Be authentic throughout the process and avoid being phony.

How to "Search" Relevant Info

How do you cull out relevant information from an ocean of info available online? The Internet has provided us access to a plethora of information, making it one of the most suitable ways to find things. However, the amount of information can also prove to be a hassle as it may take a lot of work to find something amid irrelevant and useless data. This is why one needs to learn how to search properly. This section will discuss how you can search for things and find specific information online.

Use different search engines

People generally stick to one search engine, and that's it. Do not restrict yourself to a search engine; try to use as many as possible. All search engines have one blind spot or another. Some of the most used search engines include Yahoo, Bing, and Google.

- Google is good because it has the largest page catalog and a good variety of results.
- Bing has a good autocomplete feature.
- Yahoo has a variety of search options and services.

Other search engines such as Ecosia, DuckDuckGo, and Dogpile are quite popular and have their own benefits. You can also use specialist search engines such as Google Scholar to search for specific items.

AI Prompt-based search – ChatGPT /Google Bard

chatgpt and other AI-powered search engines have immense value for teenagers' personal and professional growth. These search engines provide quick and accurate answers to a vast range of queries, allowing teens to access information on any topic, from academic research to current events.

Additionally, chatgpt and other AI-powered search engines can provide personalized recommendations and learning resources tailored to an individual's interests and learning style. This level of customization can support teens in exploring new subjects, developing skills, and pursuing their passions.

By utilizing chatgpt and other AI-powered search engines, teenagers can improve their knowledge and stay up-to-date in today's fast-paced world, contributing to their overall personal and professional growth.

Comparison:
For example, if a teenager searches for "what are the best study habits," Google might show a list of articles on the topic. However, ChatGPT and other AI prompt search engines can generate more comprehensive responses, including personalized study plans based on the teenager's learning style and preferences.

In summary, ChatGPT and other AI prompt search engines are advanced search engines that use AI algorithms to generate more personalized and comprehensive responses to user queries compared to traditional search engines like Google. These engines can provide a valuable resource for teenagers looking to learn new things, develop their skills, and pursue their passions.

Prompt Engineering- Tips

Other AI-powered search engines greatly value teenagers' personal and professional growth. These search engines :

Here are 10 tips for teenagers to search for relevant information on search engines:

1. Please be specific: You can use keywords related to the topic you are looking for to get relevant results.
2. Use quotation marks: If you are looking for a specific phrase, use quotation marks around the phrase to get exact matches.
3. Use advanced search options: Most search engines offer advanced search options that allow you to narrow down your search by date, language, file type, and more.
4. Could you check the source: Make sure the website you are getting your information from is reputable and reliable.
5. Avoid bias: Be aware of bias and try to get information from a variety of sources to avoid getting a one-sided view.
6. Use different search engines: Different search engines may have different algorithms and may give you different results. Try using more than one search engine to get a better understanding of the topic.
7. Check the date: Ensure the information you read is up-to-date and relevant.
8. Look for primary sources: Look for primary sources like research papers, government reports, and interviews to get the most accurate information.

9. Be aware of sponsored content: Some search results may be sponsored or paid for by advertisers. Please keep in mind of this, and try to avoid using sponsored content as your primary source of information.

10. Ask for help: If you need help finding relevant information, ask a teacher, librarian, or parent for help. They may have additional resources or ideas for your research.

Use Operators

You can use operators to make your search more refined.
- Use '*' as a placeholder for another word.
- Use 'OR' to search for more than one term simultaneously.
- Use "AND" to search for two or more terms.
- Type the URL of the website followed by your search keyword to search for the keyword on the website only.
- Type related: search for a website like the one you have entered in front of any website.

What is Higher-Order Thinking?

- High-order thinking can be defined as thinking on a level that is more than just saying something back to someone or memorizing facts. It is known as rote memory when someone can recall something without thinking about it. This is similar to how a robot functions, as it does not think for itself.

- Higher-order thinking, also known as HOT, allows you to think more than just restating facts.

In this kind of thinking, you need to understand the idea, connect many ideas, infer from them, categorize, manipulate, put them together, and apply them to find solutions to problems. This section will cover a variety of strategies that can help develop higher-order thinking.

Understanding importance, reasoning, and its future utility

Understanding the importance of HOT will help you understand why you should opt for it instead of rote learning.

Understand the basic concepts

Concepts of particular content areas should be identified and taught correctly. Try to understand the critical features of any specific concept properly.

Label key concepts

While understanding a topic, label and note down all the key concepts present in the case, highlight these topics, and revisit them from time to time.

Categorize concepts

Teens should be able to categorize essential concepts and understand whether an idea is concrete, verbal, nonverbal, abstract, or process.

Go from basic to sophisticated.

Once you have mastered basic concepts, you can build on them to understand more sophisticated and complex concepts. If the basic concepts are not mastered properly, you may decide to rote the complex ones, which may prove problematic later. This is especially difficult in the case of topics such as math and physics.

Discuss at Home
Teens should discuss various concepts of everyday life with their parents, teachers, and friends. It does not matter whether the subject is related directly to their studies. By discussing different ideas, you can understand the larger picture. This will make you wiser and more judicious.

Connect concepts & ideas.
Teens must learn to link one idea to another and put the ideas in order. For instance, if the concept is 'Christmas,' it can be connected to 'holidays,' which can be connected to 'celebrations.' This can help people to learn how connections are formed and how things can be connected. This can also help you develop a concrete and more refined way of thinking.

Compare
You can compare new things with what you already know. Doing this will make learning easy. Going ahead becomes easier when you can relate a new concept to something you already know. This will also help you learn more about the same topic in detail.

Learn inference
Learning inference and how one can make inferences from life and other things are necessary. For instance, if someone advises you to wear a hoodie while going out, it is cold outside. You can infer this just from the suggestion of wearing warm clothes. These inferences can be quite varied and may even seem far-fetched initially.

Teach Question-Answer Relationships (QARs)

This method is used to understand the question's nature and formulate answers.

Few Mental Models

Mental models can be frameworks that allow us to understand how the world works. Numerous mental models make studying them in a short book quite difficult. Mental models are a set of ideas and beliefs that are formed based on experiences. These beliefs can be conscious or unconscious and help us understand life and guide our behaviors and thoughts. They can be called shortcuts for reasoning. Here are some commonly used mental models.

- Backward chaining: A person is supposed to work backward from the goal.

- Anchoring: The person relies on initial information known as an anchor while making decisions.

- Classical Conditioning: Classical conditioning works on the methodology of Pavlov. In this, a biological stimulus is paired with a neutral stimulus so that the neutral stimulus can create the effects of the biological stimulus.

- Consistency and Commitment Bias: This trait reflects a desire to appear consistent and committed to whatever has been done or said.

- Comparative advantage: The ability to perform an activity better than another activity.

DID YOU KNOW?

- Did you know that higher-order thinking skills are often abbreviated as HOTS? But don't worry; it doesn't mean your brain is overheating!

- The key to having a winning mindset is to think positively. But if you can't do that, try thinking of a funny joke instead. Laughter is the best medicine, after all!

- Mental models are like filters that help us make sense of the world. Just think of them as that funny Snapchat filters you use to hide your face when you're having a bad hair day.

- If you're feeling stressed out, try using the mental model of "fake it till you make it." Just pretend you're confident, and eventually, you'll start to feel that way too!

- Higher-order thinking involves critical thinking, problem-solving, and creativity. But don't worry; you don't have to be a genius to do it. Just channel your inner MacGyver, and you'll be fine.

- The winning mindset is about setting goals and working hard to achieve them. But remember to take breaks and have some fun along the way. Life is short, after all!

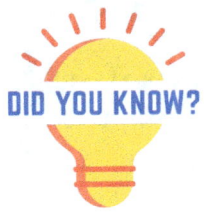

DID YOU KNOW?

- Mental models can help you make decisions quickly and efficiently. Just think of them as your brain's shortcut keys.

- Higher-order thinking skills are essential for success in school and life. But if you need help with it, remember there's always Google.

- If you want to develop a winning mindset, try adopting the mental model of "never give up." Or, if that doesn't work, remind yourself that failure is just a temporary setback on the road to success.

- Mental models can help you learn new things more quickly and easily. So the next time you're studying for a test, think of it as a mental workout for your brain!

3. THE FINANCIALLY SAVVY TEEN

A Teen's Roadmap to Financial Success

How to Make Asymmetric Money Using Creative Skill?

- Do you want to purchase the latest phone or something else you need?

- What if you could buy whatever you want using your hard-earned money?

You don't have to depend on your caregivers for monetary support. You might not be able to support yourself fully yet. You can create a side hustle to earn pocket money or build savings!

Learning to earn will improve your self-confidence, esteem, image, and respect. It will make you feel better about yourself while improving your independence. It will also teach you an essential life skill — managing money.

You don't always need a billion-dollar idea to earn. Your creative skills can help you make money in today's world. It does not matter what form of creativity you have; if you can use it efficiently, you can make money in no time. Here are a few ways to make money using your creativity.

Sell on Etsy and similar sites

Etsy is an e-commerce site that caters to creative items and products. You can sell anything from handmade home décor to vintage clothes on Etsy. It is a highly recommended website for those trying to make money using their art.

Etsy serves as an intermediary between sellers and buyers- just like eBay, except it caters more to art and creative items. It is quite easy to set up a store on Etsy. Just sign up for a new account, set up a storefront, and start listing products you want to sell.

Teach online

Various websites such as Udemy are a boon to those who want to share their knowledge with others for monetary returns. Coursera is another website where you can offer professional and creative courses to people for a small fee.

You can teach anything from languages, painting, and editing to web design. These courses are available in audio and video format and don't have to be live courses.

You can create pre-recorded videos for your students, who can view them whenever they want if they pay. The courses must be at least 30 minutes long and have at least five separate modules.

Stream Games Online

Websites such as Twitch allow users to stream their games. You may be good at playing video games and can entertain and handle an audience. If so, you can open your streaming channel on Twitch. Users can earn money in various ways on Twitch. Ads, sponsored brand placements, donations, etc., are many ways you can make money off playing video games.

Sell Printables Online

Websites such as Redbubble allow users to sell custom-designed art that can be printed on demand. You can create custom phone cases, T-shirts, mugs, posters, and other printed items on Redbubble. As the website works on a print-on-demand model, you don't have to invest much money initially. Just upload your design on the website and wait for someone to place an order. Once a product is sold, you will get royalty accordingly. You don't have to print your stuff, as Redbubble will do it for you. You upload the design, and that's it.

Click Stock photos

Websites such as SmugMug allow users to upload stock photographs that can be sold virtually and in print. SmugMug is a popular website that receives thousands of visitors every day. You can also brand the work and add a watermark to increase visibility. It can also be used as an image hosting and image-sharing website.

Publish books on Amazon

You can sell books without finding a publisher, thanks to Kindle Direct Publishing. You don't need to woo a publisher, as you can instantly release your ebook. You can price it however you want and even offer it for free. Once uploaded, the book will be available as an e-book on Kindle within 12 hours. You may not experience many sales in the first few days unless you are already an established author. But with time and proper marketing, you can sell the book quickly. Over time you will be able to collect a decent amount in no time.

Difference Between Making Money and Growing Money

If you want to improve your financial status, you must do more than earn money by doing a job or starting a business. It would be best if you learned to invest your money properly so it can grow. This may sound not easy in the beginning, but it's not. Investing money takes little time and is not as tough as it sounds. If you have a basic idea about a few things, you can easily start managing, investing, and saving your funds. If you learn to manage your funds, you're one step closer to saving and earning much money.

This chapter consists of a few tips that you can use to invest and grow your money.

Start Investing Early

The first thing you must learn about saving and investing is to start investing as early as possible. Most think you can start investing in something other than your first or second job. This is a myth. The earlier you start, the better the returns are obtained. Early investment can help you secure a better future.

Say No to Unnecessary Debt

Credit cards and loans can be extremely helpful in certain cases; however, they are a trap in most cases. You should earn and plan your finances so you don't have to repay debts. Debts generally incur much interest, which eats into your finances. Interests are nothing but unnecessary expenses that waste your crucial money. So, stop impulsive buying immediately.

Don't Put All Your Eggs in One Basket

A rookie mistake most investors make is putting all their money in a single portfolio. It is necessary to diversify your investments as it can reduce your risk of loss and improve your returns. By dividing your money, you take off the risk and allow each dividend to grow independently. Diversify for best returns and results.

Here are a few avenues in which you can choose to invest. Before deciding to invest, consult your parents or any other adult who better understands the investing market. Also, this is one of those things where you need to spend time and effort to learn and understand the markets and how they function. With the right information, you might avoid making costly mistakes.

Mutual funds
Investing in mutual funds is indeed a risky business. Still, you can earn significant profits through this medium if you understand and evaluate the risks before partaking in the avenue. You can easily invest in mutual funds if you understand the market and its risks. Mutual funds can provide a lot of profits, but you need to be bold yet informed about your investment.

Equities or Stocks
If you are okay with taking risks, investing in stocks or equities is one of the riskiest investment methods. You need to understand the share market properly and invest for the long term.

Do not be haphazard; try to be patient while investing in stocks. If you are not comfortable investing in stocks or are not aware of the fluctuating nature of the market, you should contact a professional who may help and guide you through this avenue. The share market can provide you with humongous amounts of profit if you act smart.

Invest Smartly

This is a no-brainer. It would be best if you were smart and judicious regarding your investment decisions. Knowing, understanding, and analyzing your savings plans for the future is necessary to be ready for whatever may come. Instead of investing randomly, understand the "what," "why," and "where" of your needs and choose a plan accordingly.

Without understanding the needs and requirements, you may invest in something that will not bring you any returns and, in worst-case scenarios, may even lead to huge losses.

Change Your Investments as Your Priority Changes

Change is an important aspect of life that should be followed accordingly. Change is crucial in the world of investment as well. You must prioritize your requirements and needs so that your investment suits them. If you continue to stick to one avenue of investment for a long time, you will end up in a boat stuck right in the middle of the sea and not moving anywhere. Change your investment plan from time to time, as it will increase your profits and grow your money.

Be Consistent in Your Investment

Consistency is the key as far as investment is concerned. It is necessary to be consistent as it can help you maximize your money. This is especially true in the share market and mutual funds, where being patient and consistent can help you achieve greater interest.

How to Add Value to Earn Money

Wealth is something that everyone desires. It is not a finite concept as it keeps changing constantly. The stock market fluctuates, and real estate prices go up and down. During an economic expansion, overall financial wealth also sees an upsurge. Similarly, during financial contraction and recession, overall wealth goes down.

This fluctuating quality of wealth affects how you earn, collect, and secure wealth. Learning to create wealth consistently is necessary, so your profits, revenues, and business can grow. The only way to gain wealth consistently is by learning the true source of growth of wealth and finances. This true source adds value to the world and the people of the world.

Your financial abundance and wealth depend on how much value you can create for others. So, your first goal should be to find out how to add value to the world. You start making more money when you learn how to add value to the world. But adding true value to the world means you will still need to start spending everything on charity.

It is crucial to understand how to charge others properly for the services that you provide them with. Always remember what you stand for and what direction your life is headed towards. It should be a combination of purpose, passion, and strengths. Once you have discerned your true north, you can start using it to add value to the life of people and the world in general. People will understand the value of your service or your product and will be happy to compensate you for the same.

Many believe that to help others, it is necessary to lower the value of what they provide. This means they plan to give away their services and products for a lower price or sometimes even free. This reduces the overall profit and the perceived value of a service or product, making it less popular.

When you pay little to nothing for a product or a service, you don't value it. You consider it something that can be thrown away easily. However, if you pay a sum for something, you believe it is highly valued. This way, you will use it in a much more informed manner and extract the full value of the same.

Customers, clients, and everyone, in general, think the same. If you give away your products for free for a long time, people will treat them as if it does not have any value. Using low prices is neither beneficial for the customer nor you.

Undercharging is a huge mistake and should be avoided at all costs. It is neither unethical nor morally wrong to charge people according to the product or service price. When you accept to help someone, you should be able to extract value from it.

This way, you can earn wealth by adding value to the life of people. This is one of the key bases of any business. Embrace this truth, and you are sure to succeed in your life.

Using the Leverage of Digital Space and Freelancing

Are you skilled at something? Do you want to monetize the skill to earn profit? If yes, then freelancing might be the deal for you. Unlike other methods of earning money where you have to invest and have patience, freelancing can provide almost instantaneous results.

You can get access to clients from all over the world in an online freelancing environment. With proper social, professional, and other varied skills, you can build an exceptional profile and online presence that can attract clients from all over.

It is necessary to create and build your profile properly. The more positive reviews from the clients, the more work will be done. Positive reviews will create a positive presence, making securing new jobs much easier.

Millions of people now work as freelancers full-time. It has huge opportunities and allows you to be independent while earning huge amounts.

While you can dabble in various kinds of niches in freelancing, choosing a niche that you are best at is better. This may include coding, writing, graphic design, consulting, etc. It is also possible to work in many niches, yet it is recommended to stay focused.

Some sites where you can register as a freelancer include Freelancer, Upwork, iWriter, and Fiverr.

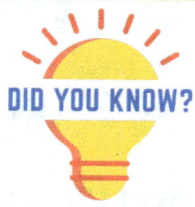

DID YOU KNOW?

- "Money" comes from the Latin word "moneta," the name of the goddess Juno in ancient Rome, who was worshipped as the protector of funds.

- If you save just $10 a week, you'll have $520 by the end of the year.

- The earlier you start saving and investing, the more time your money has to grow. For example, if you start investing $1,000 per year at age 18 and earn a 7% return, you could have over $500,000 by age 65.

- The stock market has historically provided an average annual return of around 10%. However, it's important to remember that investing always involves risk and that past performance does not guarantee future results.

- The concept of interest has been around for thousands of years. The ancient Babylonians, for example, used clay tablets to record loans with interest rates as far back as 2000 BCE.

- The first paper currency was created in China over a thousand years ago. It was originally used as a form of credit, with merchants depositing their coins with a trustworthy individual who would give them a paper receipt that could be used to claim the value of the deposit.

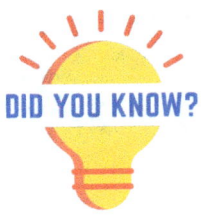

DID YOU KNOW?

- You can start investing in the stock market with as little as $10 using some mobile investment apps.

- Credit card debt can be a major financial burden, as interest rates can be high. It's important to use credit cards responsibly and pay off the balance in full each month to avoid accruing interest.

- A penny saved is a penny earned. This popular saying means that money saved is equivalent to money earned through work, highlighting the importance of saving and living within your means.

- Investing in yourself through education or skill-building can be one of the best investments. Not only can it lead to increased earning potential, but it can also lead to a more fulfilling and enjoyable career.

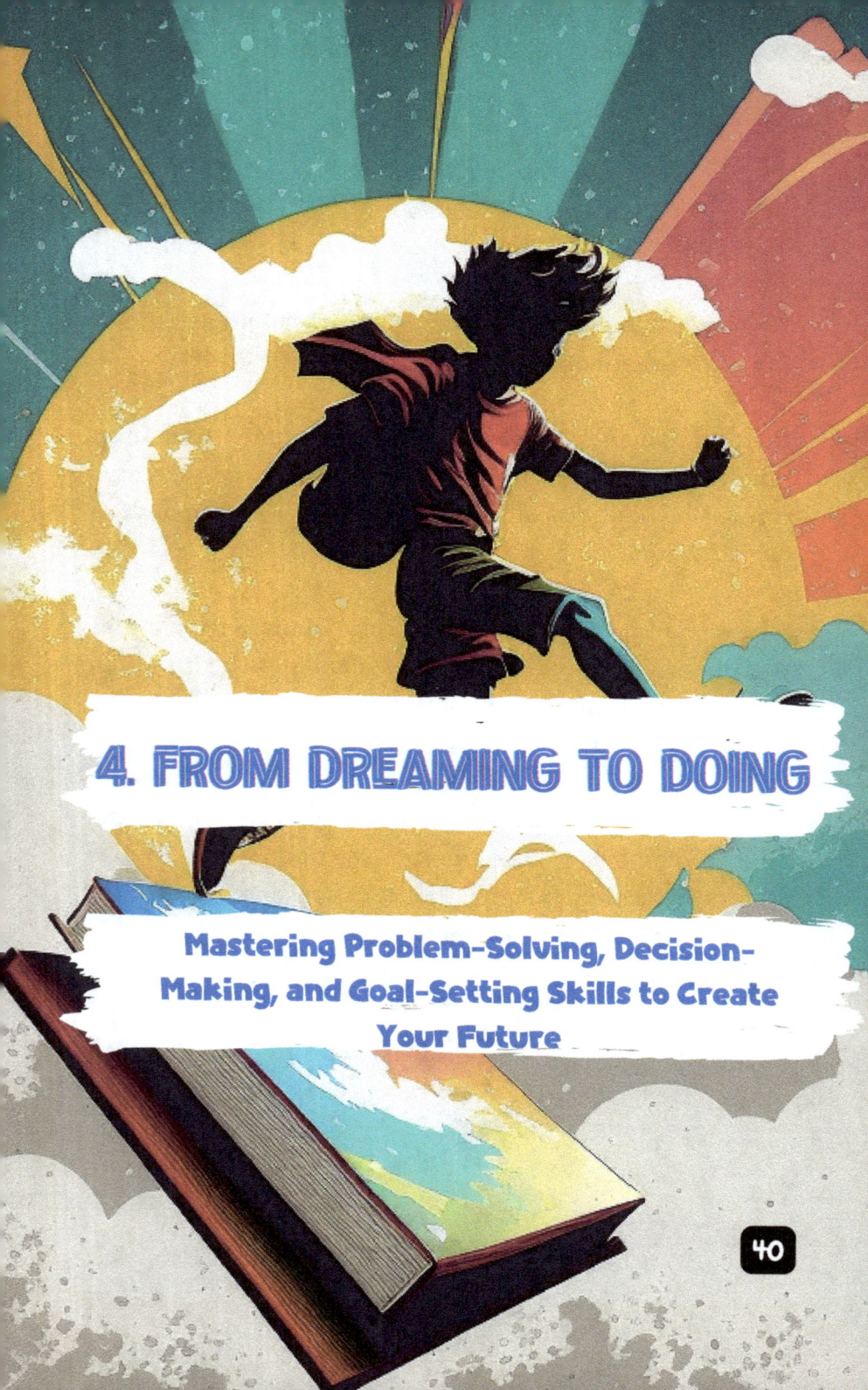

4. From Dreaming to Doing

Mastering Problem-Solving, Decision-Making, and Goal-Setting Skills to Create Your Future

PROBLEM-SOLVING

Everyone has to deal with different problems in their life. There is no such thing as a problem-free life. At times, the problem you are facing might seem like the worst thing ever. However, everything can be handled if you know what to do. Dealing with problems takes work.

It can make you feel that everything is out of your control and that you cannot do anything. It does not matter how big or small the problem is. If you don't know how to solve it and the choices to make, you may end up worsening the overall situation. Not everyone can indeed make the right choice every time. But it does not mean that you cannot even try to do so. You must learn how to be comfortable with your own decisions. Being comfortable and confident about your decisions will help in cases such as:

- You are feeling overwhelmed by the sheer number of options available.
- You are facing a difficult decision or a difficult problem.
- You want to learn how you can make better decisions.

Why problem-solving is useful

Problem-solving is helpful because it simplifies your life. It is as simple as that. If a problem is hurting you or is wearing you down, instead of wallowing in feelings of hopelessness, self-doubt, etc., solving it will help you regain control of things and feel happy and satisfied. This section will cover simple steps that can be applied to any problem to solve it.

PROBLEM-SOLVING

Everyone has to deal with different problems in their life. There is no such thing as a problem-free life. At times, the problem you are facing might seem like the worst thing ever. However, everything can be handled if you know what to do. Dealing with problems takes work.

It can make you feel that everything is out of your control and that you cannot do anything. It does not matter how big or small the problem is. If you don't know how to solve it and the choices to make, you may end up worsening the overall situation. Not everyone can indeed make the right choice every time. But it does not mean that you cannot even try to do so. You must learn how to be comfortable with your own decisions. Being comfortable and confident about your decisions will help in cases such as:

- You are feeling overwhelmed by the sheer number of options available.
- You are facing a difficult decision or a difficult problem.
- You want to learn how you can make better decisions.

Why problem-solving is useful

Problem-solving is helpful because it simplifies your life. It is as simple as that. If a problem is hurting you or is wearing you down, instead of wallowing in feelings of hopelessness, self-doubt, etc., solving it will help you regain control of things and feel happy and satisfied. This section will cover simple steps that can be applied to any problem to solve it.

8 Steps to Problem-Solving

Step 1: Define the problem

Before solving a problem, you need to understand its nature and intensity. Could you break it down and understand what it is?

Sometimes some problems may seem too big to handle. In such cases, if you break down the problem, you will be able to look at minute details of the problem and tackle them one by one. You can list all the problems and aspects of the problem to make it more manageable.

Step 2. Set some goals

Understand what the goal of your problem is. Instead of thinking about what you would like to happen, focus on what the outcomes can be.

Step 3. Brainstorm possible solutions

Be as creative as possible and try to come up with different solutions. Some ideas may seem extremely far-fetched and pointless, but don't worry; jot them down. Once you have a list of various solutions, you can move on to the next step. Keep your mind as open as possible and add all the things to the list- whether plausible or not.

Step 4: Discard any obvious wrong and poor options

Sit down and evaluate and reevaluate your list of ideas. Remove any ideas or solutions you need to be more helpful or realistic. Try to see things from a different perspective. Think how your parents or friends would handle the situation. Any option that does not involve a lot of fantasy or fiction can stay.

Step 5. Examine the consequences

Once you have gone through all the options and removed the unnecessary ones, could you make another list of all the remaining options and write down their pros and cons next to them?

Step 6. Identify the best solutions

Now let us look at all the options and begin to decide. Pick out all the practical options. Some solutions might be obvious, while others may have to be combined to find the correct path.

Step 7. Put your solutions into practice

Once you have chosen the solutions, you can incorporate them into your life and try to solve the problems.

Step 8.

How did it go? Now that you have tried out your solution, could you look over the situation? If the first solution has not worked, you may move on to the next solution. Continue this process until you come across the perfect solution.

What To Do When You Can't Fix The Issue

Sometimes some problems may prove to be difficult or downright impossible to solve. If you tried a handful of strategies and could not solve the problem, you may have to focus on coping skills instead. Coping skills will help you learn how to deal with the problem.

If the problem is causing a lot of hurt and negative feelings, it is necessary to learn how to look after yourself. Take some time for yourself to build up moral support. It would be best if you also asked for help from others. In some cases, professional help is quite useful.

DECISION MAKING

Making decisions is a challenging task. It takes much brainstorming to come to a decision or solution.

We have to make decisions all the time. These decisions can be simple and trivial such as what to have for lunch.

Or, they can be life-changing, such as what field of study to choose and to whom you should marry.

People often avoid making decisions or putting them off by searching for options, collecting a plethora of information, or asking people for suggestions. However, some people may choose to leave things to chance or take a vote. This section will deal with certain ideas that can help you learn how to make decisions with ease.

What is Decision Making?

Decision-making can be defined as the act of choosing between two or more options or courses of action. It also involves choosing between various possible solutions to any problem. These decisions can be made through reason, intuition, or a combination.

In the process of problem-solving, the process of decision-making often involves choosing between all the possible solutions to any problem.

Decisions can be made by a reasoned or intuitive process or a combination of these processes. These processes are talked about briefly below.

Intuition

Intuition is also popularly known as 'gut feeling.' In this method, you are supposed to use your intuition to choose between possible choices.

While people often talk about intuition as something magical, it combines your personal values and past experiences. It is important to consider intuition because it reflects what you have learned from your life.

An issue with intuition is that it may or may not be based on reality and may be based on your perceptions. Most of these perceptions start during childhood and may or may not be fully matured.

Thus, examining and analyzing your intuition properly is recommended so you can use it without causing any problems. Try to understand why you are feeling a certain way.

Reasonings

The reasoning is a method in which figures and facts present in front of you are used to make decisions.

The reasoning is concretely rooted in facts, which makes it ignore emotional aspects. Often, the issues from your past may affect your present decisions.

Intuition can be used to make a decision, especially if the decision is simple or needs quick action. Complicated decisions, however, should be made with the help of a more structured and formal approach. Such an approach generally involves using intuition with logic and reasoning. Ideally, you should avoid making impulsive and haphazard decisions.

Applying Both Reason and Intuition

One way to avoid impulsive decisions is to use intuition and reason together. In this method, ideally, you should use reason first to collect all the figures and facts. Once you make a list of options, you can use intuition to decide. If you feel the decision is still improper, you can move on to the next option. Check out why a certain decision can and cannot work. Suppose you are not emotionally connected and committed to a decision that you plan to make. In that case, there is a huge chance that you won't implement the decision with complete efficacy.

Effective Decision-Making

The key point in making any decision is its implementation. These decisions can be organizational, professional, or personal. This is why it is necessary to be committed to the decision rationally and personally so that you can persuade and convince others.

How to Beat Procrastination and Start Working

Maybe you need to submit a vital assignment but don't feel like doing it. So instead, you watch something on Netflix and go out to meet your friends. You feel better, but once you are home, you realize the deadline is fast approaching. Now, you feel more stressed and worried than before. Well, if you have done this, then you have procrastinated.

Procrastination is one of the biggest hindrances you may face while working on or performing any task. It is a daunting problem that affects almost everyone in this world. However, many different techniques and methods can be used to overcome procrastination. Some of these tried and tested techniques are discussed in this section.

Choose a task

One of the biggest reasons why most procrastinate is because they lack focus or have a shifting focus. We often have to do many tasks that confuse us and overwhelm us. This is why it is recommended to choose only one task or thing and focus on that particular task only. By choosing one task, you can commit to it and try to finish it before moving on to something else.

The sooner, the better

Once you have decided which task to perform, you need to act and start working on it. If you feel the task is too difficult, divide it into chunks and finish them one by one. You can also use the next method to perform difficult and time-consuming tasks.

Five Minute Method

This is one of the most effective methods to perform tasks and avoid procrastination. In the five-minute method, you need to ask yourself- 'What are the tasks or actions that I can perform in less than five minutes?'

Make a list of all the answers to this question. Then, set a five-minute timer and finish the first task on the list; similarly, finish the rest. Once you begin to do something, there is a high chance of finishing it. This effect is known as the Zeigarnik effect, in which unfinished tasks get stuck in your mind driving it in an endless loop. It would be best to remember that tiny tasks are still tasks, and finishing them takes a step toward finishing bigger tasks. Five minutes may seem a little, but they can make a difference.

Try Power Hour

Power hour or focus hour is another effective method to tackle procrastination. In this method, you must eliminate all distractions and work in intervals. For instance, you may decide to work in intervals of 20 minutes.

Work hard for 20 minutes, avoiding any distractions. After this, take a five-minute break. Once the break ends, do a focused work session for 20 more minutes. This amazing way harnesses your mind and body's optimal energy and performance. This method is also known as the Pomodoro method.

Forgiveness

Forgive yourself for procrastinating in the past, and focus on the present. This helps overcome procrastination, making you more likely to act. Try to be compassionate toward yourself and avoid lamenting or hating yourself for procrastinating in the past.

Music

Music can help you stay focused. Choose a song that makes you feel happy and energized, and play it whenever you notice yourself procrastinating. The brain will form a trigger around this song, and you will feel focused and energized whenever it is played.

Analyze

Sometimes, it is necessary to understand why you cannot focus and procrastinate while doing a particular task. Understand whether you are feeling uncomfortable, overwhelmed, bored, etc. Try to answer this question 'I'm avoiding a task because..." Identify your fears, and soon, you will see that your fears are not potent enough to stop you from doing a particular task.

Let things be

People tend to put a lot of things on their To-Do list all at the same time. If you avoid doing certain things that are not important, then remove them from the list. This means, you can focus on the important and value-adding tasks. Cross things off your list and allow yourself to let go of things.

Be accountable

Having an accountability buddy can help you stay focused and finish a task. You can also make bets with your friends regarding a particular task.

Make it enjoyable

One reason why people tend to procrastinate is they hate the task or are bored. Try to make the task and reward for its completion exciting and fun. Our brain works for rewards, and this idea can be exploited to create good habits.

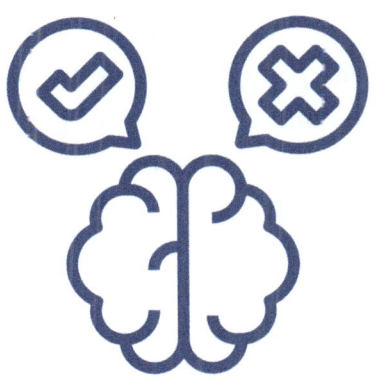

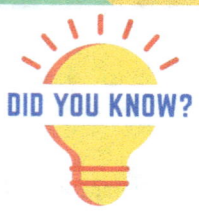

DID YOU KNOW?

- Problem-solving skills are important because they help teens to analyze complex situations, evaluate options, and find practical solutions. According to a study by the World Economic Forum, problem-solving is one of the top skills employers are looking for in new hires.

- Decision-making skills are important because they help teens to make informed choices and take responsibility for their actions. A study published in the Journal of Adolescent Health found that teens with better decision-making skills were less likely to engage in risky behaviors like substance abuse.

- Goal-setting skills are important because they help teens to focus their efforts and achieve their aspirations. According to a study published in the Journal of Educational Psychology, students who set goals and developed a plan to achieve them had higher academic performance and were more likely to complete their studies.

- One technique for problem-solving is the "5 Whys" method, which involves asking "why" five times to get to the root cause of a problem. This technique can help teens to identify the underlying issues that are causing a problem and come up with effective solutions.

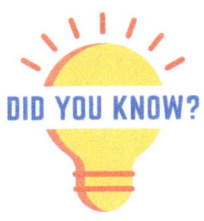

DID YOU KNOW?

- Another technique for problem-solving is brainstorming, which involves generating a list of ideas without judgment. According to a study published in the Journal of Creative Behavior, brainstorming can help teens to generate more ideas and come up with more innovative solutions.

- When making decisions, it can be helpful for teens to weigh the pros and cons of each option. According to a study published in the Journal of Experimental Psychology, individuals who weighed the pros and cons of different options made better decisions and were more satisfied with their choices.

- Another decision-making technique is the "Pareto analysis," which involves identifying the most important factors and focusing on those. According to a study published in the Journal of Medical Systems, the Pareto analysis can help individuals to make more efficient decisions.

- When setting goals, it's important for teens to make them specific, measurable, achievable, relevant, and time-bound (SMART). According to a study published in the Journal of Management, setting SMART goals can help individuals to stay motivated and achieve their desired outcomes.

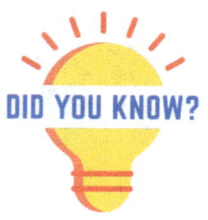

DID YOU KNOW?

- Another goal-setting technique is visualization, which involves imagining oneself achieving the goal. According to a study published in the Journal of Applied Sport Psychology, visualization can improve performance and help individuals to stay focused on their goals.

- Problem-solving, decision-making, and goal-setting skills are all interrelated, and practicing these skills can have a positive impact on a teen's personal and professional life. According to a study published in the Journal of Career Development, individuals with strong problem-solving, decision-making, and goal-setting skills are more likely to succeed in their careers and have higher job satisfaction.

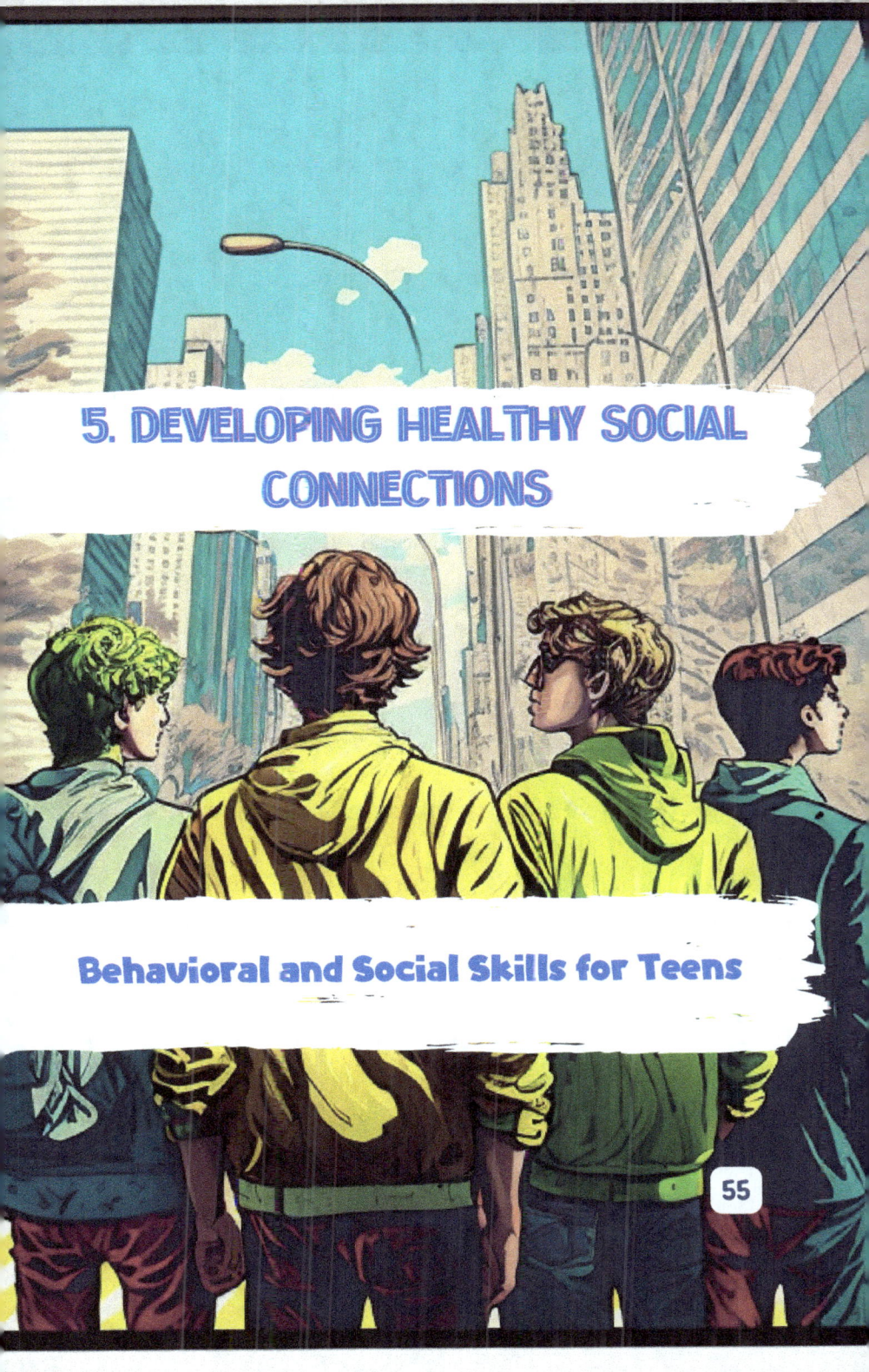

POWER OF LIKEABILITY

Were there instances when you met someone and instantly liked them?

Even if you don't meet them regularly, do you think about them favorably?

Well, this is because of their behaviors and social skills. People rarely think of how likable they are, but did you know your likability plays an important role in life?

Likable people get much more from their life than others who are not as likable. Likable people are more likely to get more job offers than others, less likely to get divorced, and more likely to keep in touch with others, including various professionals.

Here are a few tips that can help you become more likable:

Express true interest in others and what they do.

According to Dale Carnegie, one of the best ways to become more popular and likable is to show genuine interest in others and their actions.

He said a person could earn more friends within two months by showing genuine interest in the people around them. Thus, to become friendly and likable, show more interest towards others. Instead of always talking about yourself, show interest in others and listen to what they say.

Ask for help from the right people.

You can get people to like you more by asking them to help/guide you. This advice comes from Benjamin Franklin. According to Franklin, people can cooperate more if you get them to do a favor for you. A person who does a kindness for you is more likely to be kind in the next instance. Thus, you can increase the likelihood of people liking you if you get them to do something positive for you.

This scientifically tested and proven psychological phenomenon is known as the Franklin effect. People generally act in a way that focuses on their thoughts and feelings. For instance, people smile when they feel happy or cry when sad.

The reverse of this is true as well. You can make a person feel happy by making them smile. Similarly, by asking people to do a favor, they will start liking you more.

Avoid negative gossip

Gossiping is considered a way to pass the time; however, it is a double-edged sword. While gossiping can increase your likeability, in the wrong circumstances and ways, it makes you less likable. This idea is known as 'spontaneous trait transference.'

The person who gossips is associated with negativity by spreading negative gossip and ideas about others. Others will have a negative idea of you when you gossip about others by telling them negative things.

These negative traits get transferred to you, making you seem negative. When you constantly complain about someone, others will also think you are a negative person.

The reverse of this is true as well; the more positive things you say about a person, friends, colleagues, etc., the nicer and more positive you will be considered.

So, the three things that you can do to improve your likeability are:
- Showing true interest in other people.
- Asking others to do some favors for you.
- Saying positive things about other people.

How To Keep Ego side and Work For a Higher Goal

Ego can be defined as the sense of self-importance or self-esteem. Self-esteem is an integral part of any person's success. You need to believe in yourself to make anything work.

It is one of the contributing factors that make a person successful. But ego can backfire, too, especially when ego takes over everything else. While we need to trust ourselves completely, it should not prevent us from connecting and keeping up with others.
Those who can identify and overcome obstacles are much better at working with others. Suppose you feel that ego is hindering your progress, then it is time to learn how to overcome this hindrance. If so, this section contains various tips to help you grow and succeed.

You can never improve if you constantly think you are the best. It takes away any scope of becoming better and learning. Learning a new thing is hard, but it is also good for your ego as it keeps it in check and makes you humble. It also allows you to step out of your comfort zone and be open to failure and constructive criticism. It is necessary to get out of your comfort zone and try new things, which is the only way to become better and more apt leaders.

Getting out of your head

If your ego has made you overconfident in such a way that you can only think of yourself and how perfect you are, you cannot grow. Nowadays, thanks to social media, most have become self-centered and often think only about themselves.

This can hinder us from making proper decisions and moving ahead. Suppose you are too concerned about maintaining an image or are in love with a vision of yourself; it eliminates all scope of improvement.

It is necessary to take small steps toward improvement and continue to grow. Remember, no one is perfect, but you can always improve by working on yourself and getting out of your head.

Work

Remember, no good thing in this world comes easy. You must work hard to gain the success you desire. Work never ends, especially when you succeed. Real work begins when you become successful.

Silence is not always golden

When you talk about things you want to do or are planning to do, sometimes you may spend all your time and energy only talking. This means you spend more time thinking about things instead of doing them. Talking can make you feel like you are doing something important and working toward a goal. However, discussing big goals will not help you achieve them.

Our goals are big, scary, and stressful. This means we may avoid doing something because we don't feel like it. However, suppose you stop thinking and talking about your goals and start doing them. In that case, you can focus your time, energy, and effort on the task and are more likely to finish it.

Is it about the doing or the recognition?

We often prefer to think about an image of what success looks like, but it should be noted that success is not always glamorous. Instead of thinking about how success will look or feel, focus on why you want to succeed. Focus on the result and why it is necessary to do a particular task.

Be humble and be open to learning

Ego often creates a variety of problems. It can prevent you from learning and improving because it makes you think you are perfect and do not need to improve. It is necessary to keep learning and updating yourself from time to time so that you can evolve.

You can never improve if you constantly think you are the best. It takes away any scope of becoming better and learning. Learning a new thing is hard, but it is also good for your ego as it keeps it in check and makes you humble. It also allows you to step out of your comfort zone and be open to failure and constructive criticism. It is necessary to get out of your comfort zone and try new things, which is the only way to become better and more apt leaders.

Putting your ego aside and working toward bettering yourself is necessary. Like learning, work is a journey that should continue as long as you are alive. Do not let your light go out once you see some success. Be hungry for more- albeit in a positive and conducive way.

It would be best to work hard to build self-confidence, but do not let your self-confidence become arrogant. You should have confidence in yourself but never let the confidence become too inflated; otherwise, you will start ignoring others and become completely self-centered.

This narcissism does nothing good for you; it only holds you back from achieving bigger things and better success in your life. It can hold you back from becoming a better person. Confidence and ego are a thin line- you need to be confident, but never let your ego become too much.

Each person has a different definition and sense of ego. This means that how you use and leverage your ego also varies quite significantly. Understand the thin line between ego and confidence and always try to stay on the side of confidence. With the steps and ideas given above, you shall be able to become more confident and forgo unnecessary ego.

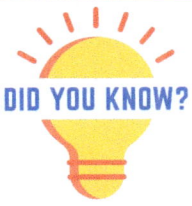

DID YOU KNOW?

- Social skills are a set of abilities that help individuals interact and communicate effectively with others. These skills can be learned and developed over time.

- Behavioral and social skills are important for teenagers as they help them build relationships, make friends, and succeed in school and future careers.

- Teens with strong social skills are better equipped to handle peer pressure, resolve conflicts, and make healthy choices.

- Developing social skills can help teens reduce feelings of loneliness, anxiety, and depression.

- Social media has both positive and negative effects on social skills. While it can help teens connect with others, it can also lead to feelings of social isolation and a decrease in face-to-face communication skills.

- Role-playing and practicing social scenarios can be effective ways for teens to improve their social skills.

- Learning to read body language, facial expressions, and tone of voice can help teens better understand social cues and respond appropriately.

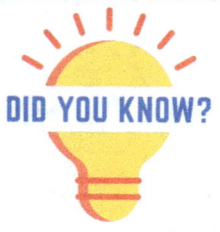

DID YOU KNOW?

- Listening actively is an important social skill that can help teens build strong relationships.

- Developing empathy and understanding others' perspectives is an important aspect of social skills for teens.

- Teaching teens to express their emotions effectively and appropriately can help them build strong relationships and communicate effectively with others.

6. HOME MAINTENANCE 101

The Skills You Need for a Happy Home

If you think that home maintenance and basic tasks are something only adults should do, you are wrong. Teens can handle many household tasks and learn how to repair basic objects. When it comes to learning, there is no such thing as being too young. Learning skills such as painting a wall, using a screwdriver, changing light bulbs, hanging a painting, etc., are basic, but they teach important life skills. These skills can help anyone learn how to maintain a house and save money by doing them independently.

This chapter comprises basic household repairs and maintenance jobs that teens can undertake.

Patching a Hole in a Wall

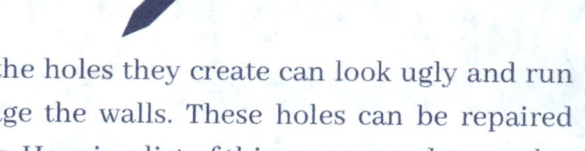

Nails and screws and the holes they create can look ugly and run down and often damage the walls. These holes can be repaired easily with a few things. Here is a list of things you need to patch a hole in the wall.

Things Needed:

- Sandpaper
- Damp Rag
- Drywall Compound
- Putty Knife

Method

- Use sandpaper to sand the rough spots around the hole.
- Wipe off dust or dirt around the hole with a damp rag. Allow the hole to dry.

- Put a small amount of drywall compound in the hole directly.
- Using a putty knife, make the surface smooth so it lays flat.
- Let it dry for a few hours.
- Sand the putty with sandpaper to make it smooth.
- If you can still see a hole, repeat the process.
- This method can fill small holes in almost all kinds of walls and is an important skill to learn.

How to Paint a Room

Painting a room may seem daunting, but it isn't. With proper tools, plans, and simple skills, anyone can paint and customize a room in no time.

Here is how you can paint a room on your own.

- Things needed:
- Painter's Tape
- Drop clothes (Old sheets are fine; however, ensure the paint does not seep through.)
- Screwdriver
- Rags
- Sandpaper
- Paintbrush
- Small bucket/ hand cups/paint tray
- Primer
- Paint
- Putty
- Paint roller and roller heads

Method

- Clean and clear the room you plan to paint. This includes removing or covering any furniture, removing things hanging on the walls, removing outlet covers and switch plates, etc.

- Put painter's tape over the sockets.

- Now fill in the unnecessary holes in the walls using the information you were introduced to previously.

- If you are painting a complete room, ceiling, and walls included, it is recommended to paint the ceiling first to avoid spillage and damage.

- To begin, prime the wall. If you are painting a new drywall over a dark color or have done a lot of healing work on the wall, it is necessary to use primer paint.

- Start with edging. With a smaller angled brush, paint all the edges. These edges include the ceiling, floor, corners, outlets, and around the windows. Try to cover at least 2-3 inches from each area. Finish the edges of one wall and then use a roller to paint the rest. Wait to start with the other walls before finishing one wall. This will help you blend the color properly and smoothly.

- In the paint tray, add some paint. Place the roller on it and roll it over the grate, so the paint is equally and evenly distributed. Now, paint the wall in large W shapes.

- After the W shapes, blend the paint on the wall with long and vertical strokes.

- When it's finished, please apply a second coat.

- Once the walls and ceiling have been painted, you can paint over any window trim or door.

- Applying multiple coats of paint is recommended for a better look and coverage. You can repeat the method in other rooms of your house.

Unblock a Gutter

It is necessary to have proper drainage in any house. Suppose you have standing or stagnant water in any part of the house; it becomes a breeding ground for mosquitoes and other insects and germs.

Also, water can leak into various parts, damaging the integrity of the property. If your home is situated amid trees that shed many leaves or needles, then cleaning the gutters from time to time is recommended to avoid any mishaps. It is also recommended to install gutter guards to protect the gutters. Here is how you can clean the gutters.

Things needed:

- Bucket
- Rubber Gloves
- Ladder

- Trash bag
- Garden hose with a sprayer attachment
- Hand trowel or a gutter cleaning tool

Method

- To start, first, detach all the downspouts. This way, you can put a bucket under the pipe, protecting other parts.

- Put on rubber gloves and use a hand trowel or a gutter-cleaning tool to remove muck and leaves. You can use your hands to clean off the large pieces. Put all the muck in either a bucket or trash bag.

- The smaller muck can be cleaned using a hose.

- Once you have removed the dirt, debris, and muck, reattach the downspouts, and with the help of a garden hose, clean the gutter again.

- Clear the ground. The ground around the downspout should be clean as well. This included trimming off the grass and removing dirt piles, rocks, etc., to ensure a free flow of water from the downspout.

- To avoid excessive clogging next time, install gutter covers that protect the gutters from large leaves and debris.

Hang a Picture

Want to hang a photo frame on the wall?

Or display your artwork?

Well, you don't have to call a handyman! You can do this! Measuring the floor's layout and space on the wall is necessary before you can hang anything on it.

This way, whatever you hang on the wall, a décor item, or a picture, will look aesthetic. Here is how you can hang a picture on a wall in your house. These tips can also be used to hang other things in your house.

Things needed:

- Pencil
- Stud finder
- Measuring tape
- Level
- Screws or nails
- Brackets, hooks, wire mounts, etc.

Method:

- Before beginning, check the placement. Do not put random holes in the walls.

- If you want to hang something heavy, install a stud. Any item above 50 lbs will surely need a stud.

- To install a stud, locate the stud using a stud finder and then adjust the setting accordingly.

- Now, measure and mark the placements where you want the studs to be. You can use sticky notes to do this.

- Measure from the top of the ceiling to the top of the picture. Now, mark the measurements with a pencil.

- With a level, check if the picture is perfectly horizontal or not.

- Finally, hammer or drill in the studs.

- Once the studs are installed, you can hang the picture. With a level, once again, could you check if the picture is straight or not?

Basic Plumbing

Basic plumbing is a skill that every person should know. Plumbers charge much money for simple tasks that can be easily managed by learning simple plumbing tasks.

Indeed, sifting through drains and toilets is not a pleasant job, but if you know to do it yourself, you can save hundreds of dollars. Think about all that you can do with the money saved!

In addition, learning how to do basic plumbing jobs can help avoid the hassle of hiring a plumber and spending a small fortune on basic repairs. You can learn the simplest things to clear up a clogged sink and toilet.

These days, information about all topics under the sun can be found online. A simple Google search will show you what you can do when facing a basic plumbing issue.

Learning the different life skills discussed in this chapter will come in handy at some point or another.

Also, if you master these skills, you can create additional income for yourself by helping the neighbors and offering your services to others around the neighborhood. So, create a side hustle while improving your skill set.

DID YOU KNOW?

- Did you know that maintaining your home can actually increase its value? Regular upkeep and repairs can prevent small issues from turning into big, expensive ones.

- The oldest known house still standing is located in what is now Israel and was built more than 10,000 years ago. It was made of mud and reeds and required regular maintenance to keep it from falling apart.

- In ancient China, the wealthy would have their homes painted in bright colors to indicate their status. However, these colors required frequent repainting and upkeep.

- The world's largest house is the Istana Nurul Iman palace in Brunei, which has 1,788 rooms and requires a team of more than 200 staff members to maintain it.

- Regular home maintenance can save you money on your energy bills. For example, sealing drafts and insulating your home can prevent heat loss, resulting in lower heating costs.

- Did you know regularly cleaning your fridge coils can help it run more efficiently and last longer? It's a simple home maintenance task that can save you money in the long run.

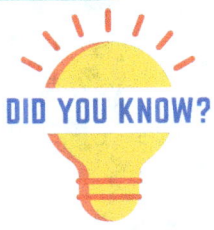

DID YOU KNOW?

- In ancient Rome, public baths were a common feature of daily life. These baths required regular cleaning and maintenance to keep them hygienic.

- The Hoover Dam, completed in 1936, requires regular maintenance to prevent damage and ensure it continues functioning properly. It's estimated that the dam requires about 24,000 gallons of paint annually to maintain its appearance.

- The simple act of replacing the batteries in your smoke detectors can save lives. It's a simple home maintenance task that can have a huge impact in the event of a fire.

- Did you know that some plants can help purify the air in your home? For example, the spider plant is known for its air-cleaning properties, so adding some greenery to your home can also be a form of home maintenance.

7. SUPER TEEN ROLE MODELS

Real Life Examples of Teens

(1) GRETA THUNBERG

Pic: Created using BlueWillow: Rights owned by creator- i.e The author
(https://docs.bluewillow.ai/bluewillow-documentation/faq)

Greta Thunberg is a well-known Swedish environmental activist who began protesting outside the Swedish parliament at the age of 15, sparking a global movement of youth climate activists.

Despite facing criticism and ridicule from some adults, Greta remains committed to her cause and has inspired millions of young people around the world to take action on climate change.

She is an inspiration for people across the globe. She has worked endlessly to help the environment and was named the person of the year for 2019 by Time Magazine.

Her hope, ideas for the future, and courage to bring about the change she believes in are inspirational for teens and adults alike.

Her motto is simple; everyone can take care of our planet, even young people. So, what are you waiting for?

(2) MALALA YOUSAFZAI

Malala Yousafzai is a Pakistani activist for girls' education who rose to prominence after surviving an assassination attempt by the Taliban at the age of 15. Malala has continued to speak out for girls' education worldwide and was awarded the Nobel Peace Prize in 2014 for her efforts. She has worked endlessly to help women gain education in Pakistan. The Taliban government shot her, but she survived and has become an advocate for women's right to education. Take a page from Yousafzai's life lesson, and don't be scared to stand up for a cause you believe in.

(3) SIMONE BILES

Pic: Created using BlueWillow: Rights owned by creator- i.e The author (https://docs.bluewillow.ai/bluewillow-documentation/faq)

She is an American gymnast who has won multiple Olympic gold medals and world championships.

She is known for her incredible athletic ability, discipline, and dedication to her sport, which has helped her overcome numerous obstacles and setbacks.

She has been open about her struggles with mental health and has taken time off from competition to focus on her well-being. By speaking out about her own experiences, Simone has helped to break down the stigma around mental health and has encouraged other young people to prioritize their mental health and well-being.

(4) JACK ANDRAKA

XPRIZE Foundation, CC BY 2.0 <https://creativecommons.org/licenses/by/2.0>, via Wikimedia Commons

Jack Andraka is an American inventor and scientist who developed a groundbreaking test for pancreatic cancer at age 15. He is known for his intelligence and creativity but also his persistence and determination in the face of challenges and setbacks.

In addition to his scientific achievements, Jack is a role model for his passion and creativity. He has shown young people the possibility of making a difference in the world by pursuing their interests and using their unique talents and abilities. He also uses his platform to advocate for science education and to encourage young people to pursue careers in science and technology.

Overall, Jack Andraka's story is a powerful reminder that young people have the potential to make a real difference in the world, and that by working hard and staying true to their passions and interests, they can achieve great things.

(5) NICHOLAS LOWINGER

When he was just a teenager, Nicholas Lowinger started taking an active part in community service that worked to provide footwear to homeless children. He also formed a nonprofit called Gotta Have Sole for the same purpose. His foundation has donated shoes to over 100,000 children in shelters across the United States. Everyone should try to incorporate his humanitarian zeal and perseverance into their life.

In addition to his philanthropic work, Nicholas is a role model for his leadership and entrepreneurial spirit. He has shown young people that it is possible to create positive change in the world by identifying a need and taking action to address it. He has also inspired others to get involved in their own communities and to use their talents and resources to make a difference in the world.

Overall, Nicholas Lowinger is a powerful example of how young people can make a positive impact by working hard, staying true to their values, and using their talents and resources to help others.

(6) Orion Jean

Orion Jean's story is inspirational to not only teens but adults too. Orion founded the organization "Race to Kindness" at the tender age of 11.

This organization held a race to 100k meals event that helped provide over 100,000 meals for free to families around the USA. In addition, this organization helped Orion become TIME's Kid of the Year for 2021. His leadership skills, combined with kindness and empathy, are something that everyone can emulate.

Orion is also a role model for his resilience and determination. He has overcome numerous obstacles in his life, including a difficult childhood and a severe illness, and has refused to let these challenges hold him back.

Overall, Orion Jean is a powerful example of how young people can positively impact the world by staying true to their passions and using their talents and resources to create positive change.

(7) Param Jaggi

Param Jaggi is a young inventor who created various devices that help the environment. His passion and zeal for the environment led him to create Algae Mobile. This device can convert carbon dioxide released from vehicles into oxygen.

Param Jaggi inspires teens because of his commitment to using science and technology to create a more sustainable future.

Param's story is a powerful example of how young people can use their passions and skills to make a difference.

In addition to his scientific achievements, Param is a role model for his commitment to education and advocacy. He has used his platform to raise awareness about environmental issues and to inspire other young people to get involved in creating a more sustainable future.

Overall, Param Jaggi is a powerful example of how young people can use their talents and passions to create a more sustainable and just world.

(8) Jasilyn Charger

Jasilyn Charger experienced mental health struggles firsthand, and her experiences led her to form the One Mind Youth Movement. This helps the youth of the Cheyenne River Sioux Tribe find resources in times of crisis.

Charger also co-founded the International Indigenous Youth Council, which has chapters across the United States of America. It helps indigenous youth and trains them in leadership to tackle the issues faced by their communities.
.
Jasilyn's story is a powerful example of how young people can use their voices and their actions to make a difference in the world.

In addition to her activism, Jasilyn is also a role model for her resilience and strength. Despite facing numerous challenges and obstacles, she has remained committed to her beliefs and has refused to back down in the face of adversity.

(9) Ryan Hreljac

By Hurljack - Own work, CC BY-SA 4.0, https://commons.wikimedia.org/w/index.php?curid=73351542

Ryan Hreljac is a Canadian philanthropist who began raising money for clean water projects in developing countries at 6. He is known for his compassion, generosity, and ability to turn his passion into action and make a real difference in the world.

He is a teen role model because of his compassion and dedication to helping others. At age six, Ryan learned that millions of people worldwide did not have access to clean water. This inspired him to take action, and he began raising money to build a well in a community in Uganda.

Through his fundraising efforts, he raised enough money to build not just one but many wells in communities across Uganda and other countries, providing access to clean water and improving the lives of countless people.

His story reminds us that we all have the power to make a difference, no matter how young or small we may feel.

(10) Zara Maria Larsson

By Photo by Stephen McCarthy/Web Summit via Sportsfile - Web Summit - https://www.flickr.com/photos/websummit/51654739994/. CC BY 2.0. https://commons.wikimedia.org/w/index.php?curid=112555971

Zara Larsson is a Swedish singer-songwriter and one of the biggest pop stars in Europe. She is known for her catchy melodies and empowering lyrics and for her work with organizations like UNICEF to promote education and equality for girls worldwide.

Zara's story is a powerful example of how young people can use their talents and passions to make a difference. Through her music, she has connected with millions of people and has used her platform to raise awareness about important issues such as feminism, LGBTQ+ rights, and mental health.

Overall, Zara Larsson is a powerful example of how young people can use their talents and passions to positively impact the world.

Quiz Time

1. What are some key life skills discussed in the book?

a) Time management, communication, problem-solving
b) Cooking, dancing, singing
c) Painting, gardening, photography

2. Why is time management an essential skill for teens to learn?

a) It helps them prioritize their tasks and stay organized.
b) It helps them become better athletes.
c) It helps them socialize with others.

3. What is the best way to approach a conflict with a friend?

a) Attack them and make them feel bad about what they did.
b) Avoid the conflict altogether.
c) Talk to them calmly and try to find a solution that works for both parties.

4. Why is communication an important skill for teens to learn?

a) It helps them express themselves clearly and effectively.
b) It helps them avoid doing homework.
c) It helps them eat healthier.

Quiz Time

5. What is the best way to deal with stress?

a) Ignore it and hope it goes away.

b) Exercise, meditate, or engage in other relaxation techniques.

c) Spend all day playing video games.

6. What are some important financial skills for teens to learn?

a) Budgeting, saving, and investing.

b) Spending all their money on clothes and shoes.

c) Taking out loans and going into debt.

7. What is the best way to deal with failure?

a) Give up and never try again.

b) Blame someone else for the failure.

c) Learn from failure and use it as an opportunity to grow.

8. Why is empathy an important skill for teens to learn?

a) It helps them understand and relate to other people's feelings.

b) It helps them get more followers on social media.

c) It helps them become more selfish.

Quiz Time

9. What are some ways to improve self-esteem?

a) Practice self-care, surround yourself with positive people, and set achievable goals.
b) Compare yourself to others and feel bad about yourself.
c) Criticize yourself and focus on your flaws.

10. Why is critical thinking an important skill for teens to learn?

a) Time management, note-taking, and test-taking strategies.
b) Cramming all night before a test.
c) Cheating on exams.

11. What is the best way to handle peer pressure?

a) Give in to the pressure and do what everyone else does.
b) Stand up for yourself and say no if uncomfortable.
c) Pretend you're sick and stay home.

12. What are some ways to improve your communication skills?

a) Listen actively, speak clearly and confidently, and use body language effectively.
b) Speak incoherently and mumble a lot.
c) Interrupt people and ignore what they're saying.

Quiz Time

13. What is the best way to approach a difficult conversation with a family member?

a) Avoid the conversation altogether.
b) Yell and scream until you get your way.
c) Approach the conversation calmly and respectfully, and try to find a solution that works for everyone.

14. What are some important study skills for teens to learn?

a) Time management, note-taking, and test-taking strategies.
b) Cramming all night before a test.
c) Cheating on exams.

15. What are some important time management strategies for teens to learn?

a) Prioritizing tasks, setting goals, and breaking down large projects into smaller steps.
b) Procrastinating and waiting until the last minute to do everything.
c) Wasting time on social media and other distractions.

Quiz Time-Answer

1. a) Time management, communication, problem-solving
2. a) It helps them prioritize their tasks and stay organized.
3. c) Talk to them calmly and try to find a solution that works for both parties.
4. a) It helps them express themselves clearly and effectively.
5. b) Exercise, meditate, or engage in other relaxation techniques.
6. a) Budgeting, saving, and investing.
7. c) Learn from failure and use it as an opportunity to grow.
8. a) It helps them understand and relate to other people's feelings.
9. a) Practice self-care, surround yourself with positive people, and set achievable goals.
10. a) It helps them analyze and evaluate information.
11. a) Time management, note-taking, and test-taking strategies.
12. b) Stand up for yourself and say no if uncomfortable.
13. a) Listen actively, speak clearly and confidently, and use body language effectively.
14. c) Approach the conversation calmly and respectfully, and try to find a solution that works for everyone.
15. a) Prioritizing tasks, setting goals, and breaking down large projects into smaller steps.

Conclusion

Thank you for choosing this book. I hope you found it informative and interesting.

Teenage is the age of new beginnings, energy, and opportunities. However, it is also the age of stress, newfound responsibilities, and trouble. Who you are in your teenage years affects whom you will become later. This is why paying close attention to your teen years is necessary to become a better person in your life later.

The life skills you learn in your teenage years will last throughout your life. These skills are essential to learning as they can help you muster enough courage and progress.

Being a teen is difficult, and no one will deny this truth, but you are not alone. Every adult you see was once a teen, just like you. So, contact your support network instead of getting overwhelmed while dealing with changes. The information you were introduced to in this book will help you make some simple and small changes that can significantly change your life. Use your teenage years wisely, have fun, and don't forget to take care of yourself!

Thank you once again.

Dr. Fanatomy

References

"5 Strategies to Get Your Ego out of the Way and Get Stuff Done." *Entrepreneur*, 5 Apr. 2018, www.entrepreneur.com/business-news/5-strategies-to-get-your-ego-out-of-the-way-and-get-stuff/311313. Accessed 8 Feb. 2023.

"5 Home Maintenance Skills Every Teen Should Learn." *Skill Trek*, 8 Feb. 2021, skilltrekker.com/5-home-maintenance-skills-for-teens/.

"10 Young People Who Changed the World to Add to Your Class Curriculum." *Waterford.org*, 9 July 2020, www.waterford.org/education/kids-who-changed-the-world/.

"10 Ways to Leverage Technology and Make Money Online." *Jammu Kashmir Latest News | Tourism | Breaking News J&K*, 29 June 2020, www.dailyexcelsior.com/10-ways-to-leverage-technology-and-make-money-online/. Accessed 8 Feb. 2023.

"A Step-By-Step Guide to Problem Solving." *Au.reachout.com*, au.reachout.com/articles/a-step-by-step-guide-to-problem-solving.

Arruda, William. "10 Steps to Getting Noticed by Thought Leaders." *Forbes*, www.forbes.com/sites/williamarruda/2016/05/10/10-steps-to-getting-noticed-by-thought-leaders/?sh=4ba89728ae19. Accessed 8 Feb. 2023.

"Effective Decision Making | SkillsYouNeed." *Skillsyouneed.com*, 2011, www.skillsyouneed.com/ips/decision-making.html.

Earp, Jo. "Developing Higher Order Thinking Skills." *Teacher Magazine*, 2 Dec. 2019, www.teachermagazine.com/sea_en/articles/developing-higher-order-thinking-skills.

Heidi. "Life Skills as High School Electives: Basic Household Repairs for Teens." *StartsAtEight*, 22 Apr. 2017, www.startsateight.com/basic-household-repairs/.

"How to Grow Money?" *Www.kotak.com*, www.kotak.com/en/stories-in-focus/how-to-grow-money.html. Accessed 8 Feb. 2023.

Kelly, Aaron. "Take Charge of Your Health: A Guide for Teenagers | NIDDK." National Institute of Diabetes and Digestive and Kidney Diseases, 16 Jan. 2019, www.niddk.nih.gov/health-information/weight-management/take-charge-health-guide-teenagers.

Le Cunff, Anne-Lauren. "30 Mental Models to Add to Your Thinking Toolbox." Ness Labs, 25 July 2019, nesslabs.com/mental-models.

Loder, Vanessa. "10 Scientifically Proven Tips for Beating Procrastination." Forbes, www.forbes.com/sites/vanessaloder/2016/04/15/10-scientifically-proven-tips-for-beating-procrastination/?sh=29d068ae296a. Accessed 8 Feb. 2023.

Mukherjee, Ritoban. "8 Ways to Make Money Online as a Creative (That You Might Not Have Thought Of)." Creative Bloq, 26 July 2022, www.creativebloq.com/features/ways-to-make-money-as-a-creative. Accessed 8 Feb. 2023.

"MindTools | Home." Www.mindtools.com, www.mindtools.com/abtrh5z/seven-ways-to-find-what-you-want-on-the-internet.

Omi, Shu. "The Power of Likeability." Shu Omi's Blog, 4 Jan. 2020, medium.com/my-learning-journal/the-power-of-likeability-ade968fb52d4. Accessed 8 Feb. 2023.

Patwal, Swati. "Personal Hygiene for Teens: Importance and Tips to Teach Them." MomJunction, 12 Dec. 2014, www.momjunction.com/articles/hygiene-tips-for-your-teens_00116170/.

Notes

Notes

www.ingramcontent.com/pod-product-compliance
Lightning Source LLC
Chambersburg PA
CBHW050320010526
44107CB00055B/2322